ACKNOWLEDGEMENTS:

Praise be to God who made all this possible. And thanks to everyone else who played a part in His divine plan. To the B.R.A.T.s (Beautiful Radiant Angel Team—Anne, Jackie, Janet, Penny, Sandy, Scarlett, Teresa, Vicky) You are my inspiration. For Rick, who lovingly puts up with all the crazy things I do and encourages me along the way, I love you dear husband! To Suzanne who was a gift from God and brought these characters to life on the pages of our books. To Bradley, whose wit and musical talents have created the theme songs for our audience. To our children who encourage me to pursue my dreams at any age. To Mary Lou and Joe who believed in me enough to help finance this venture. To Darlene and Tim for their generosity. To my mom who critiques each detail and whose talent for writing I inherited. To my Sunday School class for being my greatest fans. To all my friends who have supported, encouraged, prayed and listened to the hours of details I poured on them. I love you all! And most of all to Jesus Christ who sits beside me as I write each word on every page.
May HE receive all the honor and glory forever!

this book belongs to _____

First printing: May 2004
© 2003. All rights reserved.
No part of this book may be used or reproduced in any manner whatsoever without express
written permission of the publisher except in the case of brief quotations in articles and reviews.
For information write *Journey Stone Creations, LLC, 3533 Danbury Road, Fairfield, OH 45014*

ISBN Number: *0-9758709-0-4*
Printed in China through GlobalPSD

Please visit our web site for other great titles.
www.journeystonecreations.com

For information requesting author/illustrator interviews, please contact us at 513-860-5616
or e-mail *pat@journeystonecreations.com*

the A.W.A. gang

ANGELS WITH ATTITUDES!

IN THE BEGINNING...

Written By Patricia Stirnkorb

Illustrated By Suzanne Bock

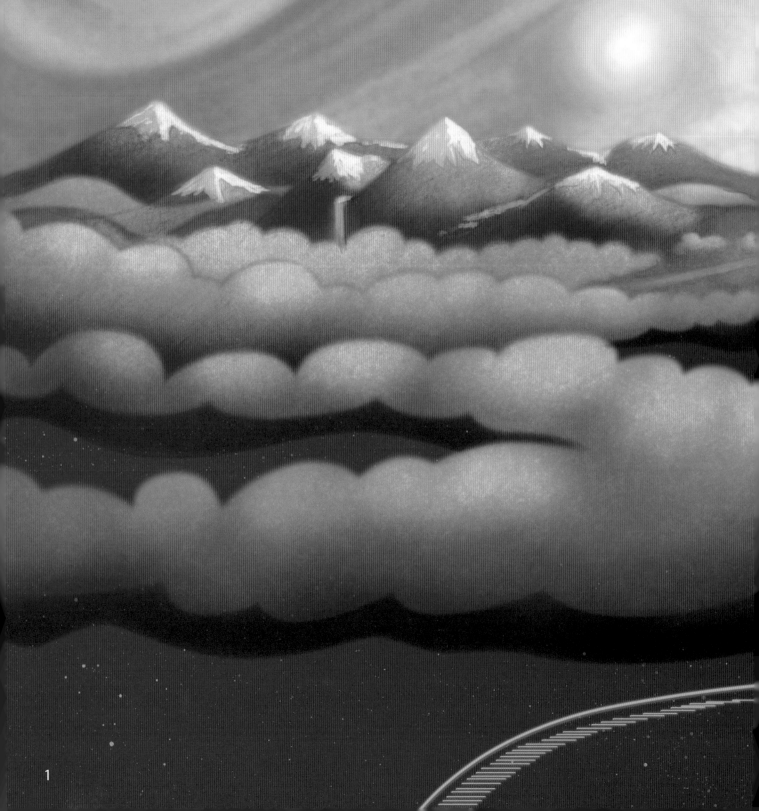

This is a story about a group of children. Not just any children. These are earth angels. Most of the time they live in heaven, but occasionally they come to earth to work, to protect, or to help earth kids learn a lesson. They call themselves the A.W.A. Gang – Angels with Attitudes. And this is the story about how they got their name...

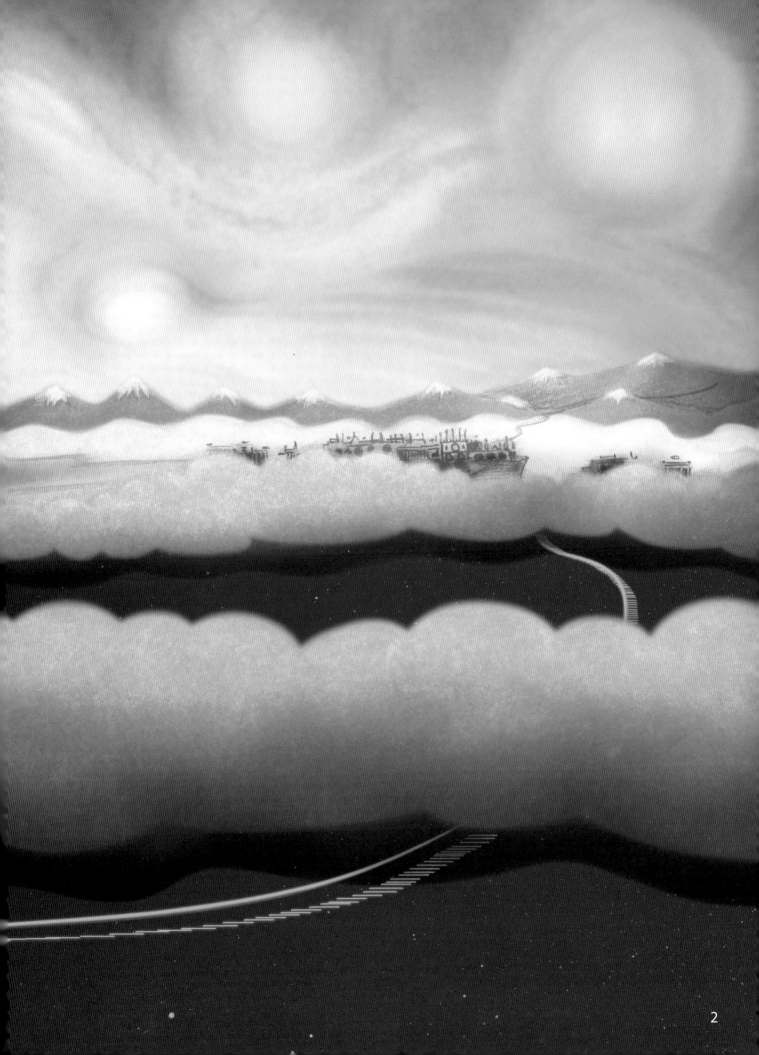

Patrick, Kevin, Andy, Ray and Thomas were standing at the corner of Crystal and Sapphire streets talking about "guy" things when along came Bonnie, skating ahead of her friends who were on foot, Exxie, Anne, and Chrisy. Suddenly Bonnie hit a rock and toppled right in the center of the boys!

"Oops! Sorry!" She cried as she scrambled to gather her wits and white robe from around her tangled legs. "I didn't mean to do that, honest!"

"Girls are such klutzes!" said one of the boys.

"Yeah, they can't do anything right," said another.

"If I had roller skates, I'd teach you how to skate," said Andy.

"Hey, I know how to skate! And better than any of you! I said I was sorry. I hit a rock or something!" Bonnie shouted in her own defense, just as the rest of the girls made their way to the gang.

"What's going on?" Chrisy asked.

"Nothing." They all mumbled in unison.

"What's everyone doing?" Exxie asked. "Let's go for a walk and do some exploring!" She went on excitedly.

"No thanks! No more walks! We've seen everything! NO!" Andy was usually the first to voice his opinion.

"Well," said Kevin, "We could practice singing. I know I have my bells in here somewhere." His voice trailed off as he dug through the pockets of his robe. All he found were candy wrappers and half-eaten candy bars. He could hear them ringing, but couldn't quite put his hands on them.

"No thanks! I hate singing more than I hate exploring!" Andy replied.

"Well, what do you want to do?" asked Patrick.

The kids began to discuss their options and were so engrossed in their conversation that they didn't hear the group of adult angels approaching. The adult angels, also deep in talk, barely noticed the kids.

Ray and Exxie stopped talking just in time to overhear one of the adults say something about the need for more "earth angels." Everyone wanted to be an earth angel – especially the kids! That is probably because it is very, very rare that a child angel ever gets to go to earth.

"Excuse me," Exxie tugged at the robe of one of the adults. "Did you say you need more earth angels? We could do it for you, we could be the extra ones you need."

With that, all the kids stopped talking and looked at the adults.

"I don't think so!" said Martha, one of the adult angels.

"Absolutely not!" laughed another adult named Wendy.

"Not hardly!" said James and Andrew, almost at the same time. James is one of the archangels, and he usually hands out the assignments to helper angels.

"That would require so much approval and special permission and extra work ... no, not a possibility," said Michael, the head archangel and leader of all the heavenly angels.

By now all the rest of the angel kids had gathered around the adults. They all chimed in at once.

"We could do it! We'll help you get permission!" Exxie exclaimed.

"Yeah, let us go! We'd be great!" said Ray.

"We work together quite well," said Patrick, self-appointed leader of the kids.

"We can do it!" said Chrisy, the scholar of the group and always the first to answer with a quotation. "God will give us the wisdom to do it!"

"I can fix their hurts," said Thomas, reaching for his first aid kit.

"Please!" they all cried at once.

"And I can teach the earth kids to skate!" Bonnie said as she skated around the whole ring of angels, just to show her skills. She was very good because she loved to skate and almost never took her skates off!

But the adult angels were not impressed.

"We've seen you bickering with one another. And most of you have
been caught walking across the Crystal Sea instead of using the silver
stepping-stones. You've even been caught sliding down the golden banister.
I don't know – you all have attitudes!" Michael told the kids. They were
very quiet and no one said a word, each hanging their head, and nodding
in agreement.

"We don't always bicker," Patrick said finally. "We really love each other
and support one another. We play together very well – most of the time."

"And that is another point," Michael said. "This is not play. It's very
serious work. I'm just not sure you are ready for it."

He looked at the other adult angels. James nodded in agreement.
Everyone was silent.

"But they have to learn somehow," said Wendy as she shrugged her shoulders. "It might be an educational process for them."

"But what if they, you know, mess up?" James asked with concern.

"Well, we would have to give them assignments that aren't so sensitive..." Wendy said thoughtfully.

"I guess if we could get special permission, they would be a great help to us," Martha said.

"And think, nine more earth angels. Even if they are angels with attitudes," Andrew said with a smile.

"I guess I can check with the Big Guy and see what He thinks. I'll let you know tomorrow. Meet us back here at this same place, 8 a.m. sharp." James said. Then he and the other adults continued on their path, talking in low voices that the kids couldn't hear.

"Wow! Earth Angels!" Anne was very excited about that. As the smallest and quietest of the gang, she rarely spoke. However once she got started, watch out, she could hold her own in any argument. Anne was generally late for everything; but she had a heart of gold when it came to helping others.

"I think we should pray about it," said Chrisy, the self-appointed chaplain of the group. She pulled out her Bible, flipped to a page and read. "'Commit your work to the Lord and your thoughts will be established.' Proverbs 16:3. We can do this, as long as God helps us out!"

"Well, I'm ready," said Andy.

"Me too," Patrick replied.

"What do you think Kevin?
It's almost enough to make
us all sing!"

Kevin answered by ringing
his bells. His mouth
was full of candy!

At exactly 7:45 a.m. the next day, the kid angels were waiting on the same corner where they had met the adults the previous morning. They were discussing their possible assignments before James arrived.

"Maybe we are going to visit with a sick earth child," said Thomas, lifting his first aid kit in the air.

"No, they wouldn't send us for that..." Bonnie replied. "Maybe it will be to help kids learn about being good sports. Like ball players or skaters or something."

"Oh, brother," said Andy. "Is that all you think about? I bet it is to help some old person or something boring. That's why they wanted adult angels instead of kids."

"I don't care what we have to do," said Exxie. "I just can't wait to explore earth."

"Well, I think we need a name," said Ray. "What can we call ourselves?"

"What about a sports name? Like the Yankees, the Reds, or the Astros..." Patrick said, thinking out loud.

"No, that's dumb," said Andy. "There are already teams with those names. We need something different.

"Yea, something, you know, Heavenly," said Chrisy.

"I agree," said Anne.

"Well, what are we?" asked Kevin. "We are protectors, messengers, guardian angels. We need our name to say who we are, and what we do."

"I've got it," said Ray. "Each of us should write down a name that we think would fit us and what we do, and we can put it all together and compare notes."

Kevin jumped up and quickly searched through his very large pockets.
He passed out paper and pencils as everyone found a place to sit down. Each
of the kids thought about the job they would do on earth.

"Okay, who wants to go first?" asked Patrick.

"I will, I will! How about the Braves?" answered Bonnie.

"Oh yeah," said Andy, "Exxie and Anne are afraid of their own shadows."

"Well what have you got, smarty?" Bonnie replied.

"How about just keep it simple – Angels. We can just be the Earth Angels," Andy said.

"Well, I wrote down Reliable," said Ray. "You know Michael pointed out that it is a big responsibility. We have to be reliable."

"That's true," said Thomas. "But what about Team Angels? That kind of says it all. We are a team, at least most of the time. And Andy is right, we are just angels. What do you think of that?"

"I think we are Awesome," said Anne. "How about the Awesome Angels?"

"Oh, brother," said Andy, rolling his eyes. "Who else has something?"

"I wrote down Protectors," said Patrick. "We will be protectors..."

"Well, aren't we forgetting who is really amazing here? It isn't us, gang! I think we should be Courteous. You know, polite. The Courteous Kids," Chrisy said.

"How about just Kids?" said Kevin. "We are just kids you know."

"Well, what if we don't have a name, just a symbol or a sign?" asked Exxie. "You know, like, well, how about an exclamation point! How would that be?"

"Dumb, dumb, dumb," said Andy, shaking his head.

Just then, James and Martha approached the kids.

"What's going on?" James asked.

"We are trying to come up with a name
we can all agree on for our earthly
assignments," Patrick explained. "But we
can't seem to agree on anything!"

"That's because what you really are, is a gang of angels with attitudes!" said James. "The Angels with Attitudes Gang! That should be your name!" "Hey," said Patrick. "I like that—What about the A.W.A Gang? Angels with Attitudes!"

"I was kidding!" said James. "I was only kidding! But, you know, I kind of like that..."

And so it was, the A.W.A. Gang was created – The Angels with Attitudes Gang.

"And by the way," said James. "I have your first earth assignment. But you all have to follow Martha to get your equipment. Then tomorrow you'll leave for earth."

There were lots of questions on the minds of each of the angels as they followed Martha to the equipment room. Where would they go? What would they wear? What would happen to their wings? They would be assigned a special backpack to protect their wings and halos while on earth. It would hold their Little Lights, their Journey Stones to get them back to heaven, and even some stars to sprinkle in the eyes of an earth child that needed to see the good in others.

And James knew that if everything worked out, not only was the A.W.A. Gang going to help the earth kids, but they would also learn a lot of lessons for themselves.

NOTE FROM THE AUTHOR AND ILLUSTRATOR:

We hope you have enjoyed reading about the A.W.A.Gang
and want to learn more about their earthly adventures.
Please watch for the following titles in this line:

Here Kitty

Big Bad Bully

Treasure Found

A Place for the King (Christmas story)

Meet the Angels

This Little Light

When we began this project, Suzanne said
"If just one child desires to learn more about God or Heaven because
of these books, then all our hard work will have been worth it."
It is our desire that all children should know the story of God.

Parents, if your child or children have questions about God, Christ or Heaven after reading one of our books,
please go to our web site at www.journeystonecreations.com and check out the Parents page.
This helpful information will provide a way to discuss these topics with children.